ENGLISH TOWN

FOR EVERYONE

STARTER

BOOK 2

Contents

Characters

Hello Song

Hello, everyone.
Hello, teacher!
Hello, friends!

Let's have fun together.
We'll have a good time.

Are you ready to start?
We're ready!

Here we go!

Goodbye Song

Did you have fun?

It's time to say goodbye.
See you next time!
See you next time!

Did you enjoy the class?
Yes! We had a fun time!
Yes! We had a fun time!

See you later! See you later!
Goodbye. Goodbye.

Bye! Bye!

Lesson 1

Time

 Talk 1

A. Look, listen, and repeat.

Wake up!

Okay, Sally.

Say and Act

Wake up!

Okay, Sally.

6

B. Listen, circle, and say.

1 **ⓐ**  **ⓑ**

2 **ⓐ**  **ⓑ**

 **Talk 2**

A. Listen and sing.

What Time Is It?

Tick-tock, tick-tock.
Wake up! Wake up!
Okay! Okay!
What time is it?
It's eight o'clock.

Tick-tock, tick-tock.
Wake up! Wake up!
Okay! Okay!
What time is it?
It's nine o'clock.

B. Look, listen, and repeat.

What time is it?

It's eight o'clock.

C. Listen and point. Make sentences.

It's _____ o'clock.

1 **6**
six

2 **7**
seven

3 **8**
eight

4 **9**
nine

5 **10**
ten

A: What time is it?
B: It's _____ o'clock.

D. Listen, point, and say.

 Talk 1

A. Look, listen, and repeat.

It's time for school.

Oh, no. I'm late.

It's time for school.

Oh, no. I'm late.

B. Listen, match, and say.

1  • •

2  • •

 **Talk 2**

A. Listen and sing.

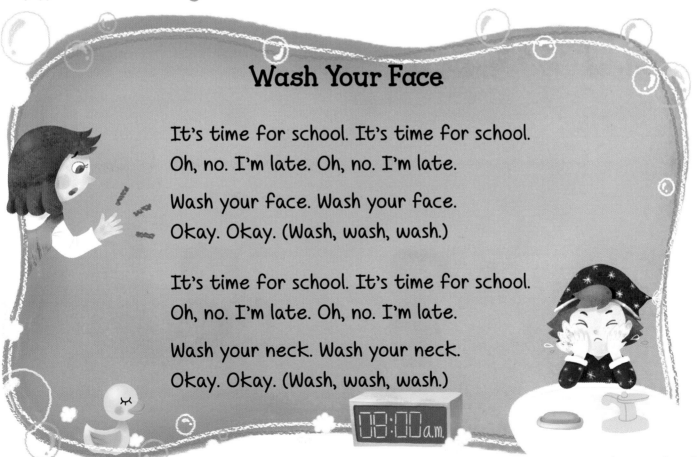

Wash Your Face

It's time for school. It's time for school.
Oh, no. I'm late. Oh, no. I'm late.

Wash your face. Wash your face.
Okay. Okay. (Wash, wash, wash.)

It's time for school. It's time for school.
Oh, no. I'm late. Oh, no. I'm late.

Wash your neck. Wash your neck.
Okay. Okay. (Wash, wash, wash.)

Wash your face.

Okay.

e-learning

C. Listen and point. Make sentences.

Wash your _____.

1

face

2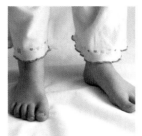

feet

3

hands

4

neck

A: Wash your _____.
B: Okay.

D. Listen, point, and say.

Phonics

-am, -an, -ap, -at

 Phonics Time

A. Look, listen, and repeat.

-am

h**am**   j**am**

-an

c**an**   f**an**

-ap

m**ap**   n**ap**

-at

h**at**   m**at**

e-learning

B. Listen and chant.

Let's say am, am, am

am am ham ham ham

am am jam jam jam

Let's say an, an, an

an an can can can

an an fan fan fan

Let's say ap, ap, ap

ap ap map map map

ap ap nap nap nap

Let's say at, at, at

at at hat hat hat

at at mat mat mat

C. Find and circle. Read along.

A boy with a hat is on a mat.
He takes a nap with a map.
A can is on a fan.
A ham is on top of jam.

Fun Time

3 feet

2 Wash your neck!

4 Next time!

5 Let's sing on page 7.

6
A: What time is it?
B: _____

11 Return to Start!

12 It's eight o'clock.

13 Go back to 3.

14 A: _____
B: It's nine o'clock.

Start

1 A: _____
B: Okay.

7 It's time for school.

8 A: It's time for school.
B: _____

9 A: _____
B: Okay.

10 Let's sing on page 11.

Finish

15 Wash your neck.
Wash your feet.

Lesson 4 Feelings

 Talk 1

A. Look, listen, and repeat.

Are you okay?

No, I'm not.

 Say and Act

Are you okay?

No, I'm not.

B. Listen, check, and say.

1 **ⓐ**  ☐

ⓑ  ☐

2 **ⓐ**  ☐

ⓑ  ☐

 **Talk 2**

A. Listen and sing.

What's Wrong?

Are you okay? Are you okay?
No, I'm not. No, I'm not.
What's wrong? What's wrong?
I'm tired. I'm tired.

Are you okay? Are you okay?
No, I'm not. No, I'm not.
What's wrong? What's wrong?
I'm sleepy. I'm sleepy.

B. Look, listen, and repeat.

What's wrong?

I'm tired.

e-learning

C. Listen and point. Make sentences.

I'm _____.

1

angry

2

sad

3

sleepy

4

tired

D. Listen, point, and say.

A: What's wrong?
B: I'm _____.

Lesson 5 Symptoms

 Talk 1

A. Look, listen, and repeat.

How do you feel today?

I'm sick.

How do you feel today?

I'm sick.

B. Listen, number, and say.

 ☐

 ☐

 ☐

 ☐

 **Talk 2**

A. Listen and sing.

How Do You Feel Today?

How do you feel today?
How do you feel today?
I'm sick. I'm sick.
Do you have a fever?
Do you have a fever?
Yes, I do. Yes, I do.

How do you feel today?
How do you feel today?
I'm sick. I'm sick.
Do you have a cold?
Do you have a cold?
Yes, I do. Yes, I do.

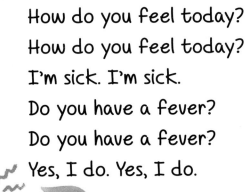

Do you have a fever?

Yes, I do.

C. Listen and point. Make sentences.

Do you have a _____?

1

cold

2

fever

3

headache

4

toothache

A: Do you have a _____?
B: Yes, I do.

D. Listen, point, and say.

6

Phonics

-ed, -en, -et, -est

Phonics Time

A. Look, listen, and repeat.

bed

red

hen

pen

net

wet

nest

vest

B. Listen and chant.

Let's say ed, ed, ed
ed ed bed bed bed
ed ed red red red

Let's say en, en, en
en en hen hen hen
en en pen pen pen

Let's say et, et, et
et et net net net
et et wet wet wet

Let's say est, est, est
est est nest nest nest
est est vest vest vest

C. Find and circle. Read along.

A red hen is on a bed.
She wears a wet vest.
A red pen is in a net.
Eight eggs are in a nest.

Fun Time

1
A: _____
B: I'm tired.

7
A: How do you feel today?
B: _____

Start

8 Return to Start!

9 Are you okay?
☐ No, I'm not.
☐ Yes, I am.

10
A: _____
B: Yes, I do.

Finish

15
A: Do you have a headache?
B: _____

Days of the Week

 Talk 1

A. Look, listen, and repeat.

Be quiet.

I'm sorry.

Be quiet.

I'm sorry.

B. Listen, circle, and say.

 Talk 2

A. Listen and sing.

What Day Is It Today?

Be quiet. Be quiet.
I'm sorry. I'm sorry.
Be quiet. Be quiet.
I'm sorry. I'm sorry.

What day is it today? What day is it today?
Monday, Tuesday, Wednesday, Thursday,
Friday, Saturday, and Sunday.
It's Monday. Monday.

What day is it today?

It's Monday.

e-learning

C. Listen and point. Make sentences.

It's _____.

1 MONDAY — Monday

2 TUESDAY — Tuesday

3 WEDNESDAY — Wednesday

4 THURSDAY — Thursday

5 FRIDAY — Friday

6 SATURDAY — Saturday

7 SUNDAY — Sunday

A: What day is it today?
B: It's _____.

D. Listen, point, and say.

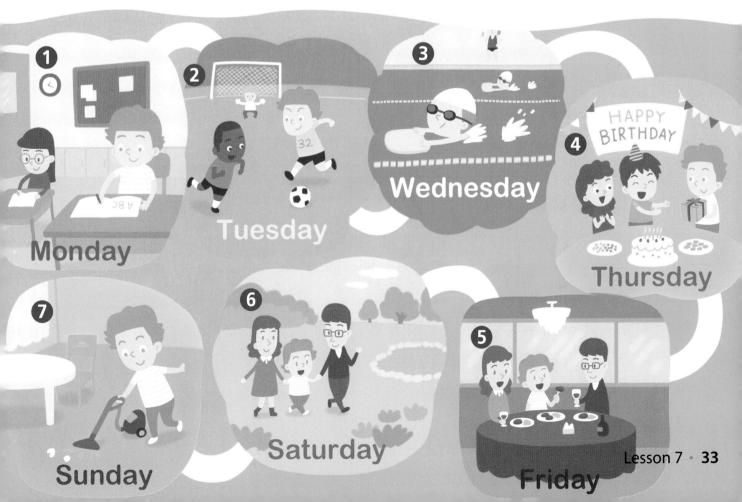

Monday

Tuesday

Wednesday

Thursday

Friday

Saturday

Sunday

HAPPY BIRTHDAY

Lesson 7 · **33**

Lesson 8 Subjects

 Talk 1

A. Look, listen, and repeat.

Don't run!

Okay.

B. Listen, number, and say.

 **Talk 2**

A. Listen and sing.

Don't Run!

Don't run! Don't run! Okay. Okay.
Don't run! Don't run! Okay. Okay.

M-O-N Monday. Monday! Monday! Today is Monday!
I like Monday! We have music class.
T-U-E-S Tuesday. Tuesday! Tuesday! Today is Tuesday!
I like Tuesday! We have art class.

B. Look, listen, and repeat.

Today is Monday.

I like Monday.
We have music class.

e-learning

C. Listen and point. Make sentences.

I like Monday.
We have _____ class.

1

art

2

math

3

music

4

P.E.

D. Listen, point, and say.

A: Today is Monday.
B: I like Monday. We have _____ class.

3 + 4 =
15 - 9 =

Phonics
-ig, -in, -it, -ix

 Phonics Time

A. Look, listen, and repeat.

-ig

b**ig**   w**ig**

-in

b**in**   p**in**

-it

h**it**   s**it**

-ix

f**ix**   m**ix**

B. Listen and chant.

Let's say ig, ig, ig

ig ig big big big

ig ig wig wig wig

Let's say in, in, in

in in bin bin bin

in in pin pin pin

Let's say it, it, it

it it hit hit hit

it it sit sit sit

Let's say ix, ix, ix

ix ix fix fix fix

ix ix mix mix mix

C. Find and circle. Read along.

They are my mom and dad.
He has a big wig.
He has a big pin.
He can sit and fix a bin.
She can hit and mix eggs.

Assessment Test 1

🎧 **Listening**

A. Listen and check.

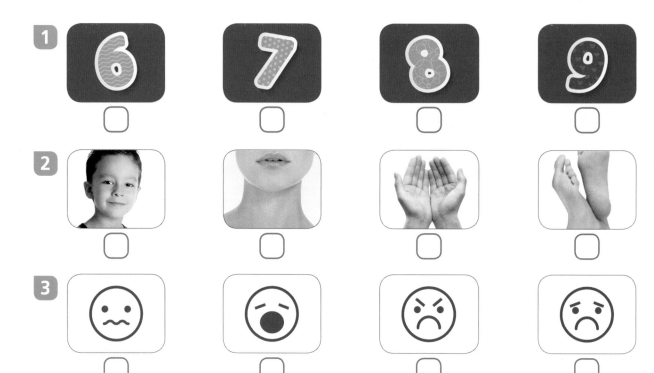

B. Listen and choose O or X.

C. Listen and circle.

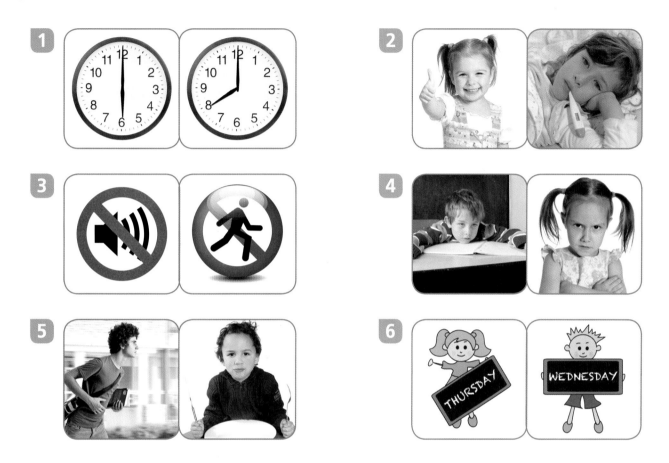

D. Listen and number.

Reading Read and number.

1. We have P.E. class.
2. It's Monday.
3. Wash your neck.
4. I'm sick.
5. I'm sleepy.
6. Don't run!

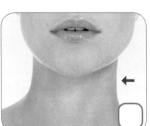  

 Writing Match and trace.

1  • • It's Tuesday.

2  • • Wash your hands.

3  • • I'm sad.

4  • • It's time for school.

44

 Speaking

A. Listen, point, and answer.

B. Listen and answer.

1

2

3

4

Cafeteria

A. Look, listen, and repeat.

Get in line.

Okay.

B. Listen, check, and say.

1 ⓐ    ⓑ

2 ⓐ    ⓑ

 **Talk 2**

A. Listen and sing.

What Do You Want?

Get in line. Get in line. Okay. Okay.

What do you want? What do you want?
Chicken. Chicken. I want chicken.
Chicken. Chicken. I want chicken.

Get in line. Get in line. Okay. Okay.

What do you want? What do you want?
Bread. Bread. I want bread.
Bread. Bread. I want bread.

What do you want?

I want chicken.

C. Listen and point. Make sentences.

I want _____.

bread

chicken

fish

rice

D. Listen, point, and say.

A: What do you want?
B: I want _____.

Lesson 12 — Team Sports

 **Talk 1**

A. Look, listen, and repeat.

Look at this, Mark!

Wow, it's a soccer ball!

B. Listen, match, and say.

 Talk 2

A. Listen and sing.

Let's Play Soccer

Look at this, Tom!
Wow, it's a soccer ball!
Let's play soccer.
Let's play soccer.
Okay. Okay.

Look at this, Jane!
Wow, it's a basketball!
Let's play basketball.
Let's play basketball.
Okay. Okay.

B. Look, listen, and repeat.

Let's play soccer.

Okay.

e-learning

C. Listen and point. Make sentences.

Let's play _____.

badminton

baseball

basketball

soccer

A: Let's play _____.
B: Okay.

D. Listen, point, and say.

Phonics

-og, -op, -ot, -ock

Phonics Time

A. Look, listen, and repeat.

frog   **l**og

hop   **m**op

hot   **p**ot

rock   **s**ock

B. Listen and chant.

Let's say og, og, og   og og frog frog frog

                     og og log log log

Let's say op, op, op   op op hop hop hop

                     op op mop mop mop

Let's say ot, ot, ot   ot ot hot hot hot

                     ot ot pot pot pot

Let's say ock, ock, ock   ock ock rock rock rock

                     ock ock sock sock sock

C. Find and circle. Read along.

A frog is on a log.
He can hop with a mop.
A dog is on a rock.
She can hop with a sock on.
A fox is on a box.
He can hop with a hot pot.

 **Play**

A. Listen and chant.

Let's Play Baseball

What do you want?
What do you want?
Rice, rice. I want rice.
What do you want?
What do you want?
Fish, fish. I want fish.

Let's play baseball.
Let's play baseball.
Sounds good.
Let's play badminton.
Let's play badminton.
Okay. Yeah!

B. Play a game.

A: What do you want?
B: I want fish.

A: Let's play soccer.
B: Okay.

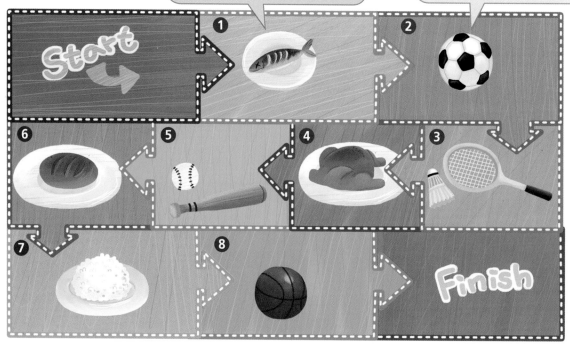

Start

① ②

⑥ ⑤ ④ ③

⑦ ⑧ Finish

Reading Time

Foods around the World

Look at this! It's pasta.
It's an Italian food.

Let's have a taco.
It's a Mexican food.

What about this one?
It's naan. It's an Indian food.

Oh, all of these look delicious.
Which do you want?

Read and check.

1. What is Mexican food?　　　ⓐ a taco　　　ⓑ naan

2. What is pasta?　　　ⓐ Indian food　　　ⓑ Italian food

Lesson 14

Playground

A. Look, listen, and repeat.

How old are you?

I'm eight years old.

Say and Act

How old are you?

I'm eight years old.

B. Listen, draw, and say.

 **Talk 2**

A. Listen and sing.

Who's That?

How old are you?
I'm eight years old.
How old are you?
I'm nine years old.

Who's that? Who's that?
He's my coach. He's my coach.
Who's that? Who's that?
She's my friend. She's my friend.

B. Look, listen, and repeat.

Who's that?

He's my coach.

e-learning

C. Listen and point. Make sentences.

He's/She's my _____.

1

coach

2

friend

3

student

4

teacher

A: Who's that?
B: He's/She's my _____.

D. Listen, point, and say.

Lesson 15

Cold Drinks

Talk 1

A. Look, listen, and repeat.

I'm thirsty.

Let's drink some water.

I'm thirsty.

Let's drink some water.

B. Listen, check, and say.

1   ⓐ    □   ⓑ    □

2   ⓐ    □   ⓑ    □

 **Talk 2**

A. Listen and sing.

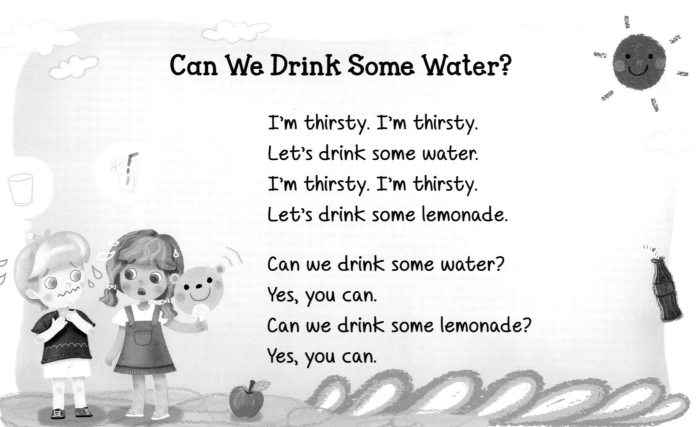

Can We Drink Some Water?

I'm thirsty. I'm thirsty.
Let's drink some water.
I'm thirsty. I'm thirsty.
Let's drink some lemonade.

Can we drink some water?
Yes, you can.
Can we drink some lemonade?
Yes, you can.

Can we drink some water?

Yes, you can.

C. Listen and point. Make sentences.

> Can we drink some _____?

1

apple juice

2

coke

3

lemonade

4

water

> A: Can we drink some _____?
> B: Yes, you can.

D. Listen, point, and say.

Phonics

-ub, -ug, -un, -up

 Phonics Time

A. Look, listen, and repeat.

-ub

cub   **tub**

-ug

mug   **rug**

-un

bun   **sun**

-up

cup   **pup**

B. Listen and chant.

Let's say ub, ub, ub

ub ub cub cub cub
ub ub tub tub tub

Let's say ug, ug, ug

ug ug mug mug mug
ug ug rug rug rug

Let's say un, un, un

un un bun bun bun
un un sun sun sun

Let's say up, up, up

up up cup cup cup
up up pup pup pup

C. Find and circle. Read along.

Can you see a cub?
The cub is in a tub.
Can you see a pup?
The pup is on a rug.
Can you see a bun?
The bun is in a mug.
Can you see the sun?
The sun is in a cup.

 **Play**

A. Listen and chant.

Can We Drink Some Apple Juice?

Who's that? Who's that?
She's my student. She's my student.

Can we drink some apple juice?
Can we drink some apple juice?
Yes, you can. Yes, you can.

Who's that? Who's that?
He's my teacher. He's my teacher.

Can we drink some coke?
Can we drink some coke?
Yes, you can. Yes, you can.

B. Play a game.

A: Who's that?
B: He's my friend.

A: Can we drink some water?
B: Yes, you can.

68

Reading Time

e-learning

Camels in the Desert

What's that? It's a camel.

Camels are in the desert.

They can walk for weeks without water.

They get energy from their humps. Isn't that surprising?

Read and check.

1. Can camels walk for weeks without water?

    a Yes, they can.   **b** No, they can't.

2. Where do camels get their energy from?

    a their tail   **b** their humps

Lesson 17 Body Parts

A. Look, listen, and repeat.

Look at him!

Wow, he's so fast!

Say and Act

Look at her!

Wow, she's so fast!

B. Listen, match, and say.

1  • •

2  • •

 **Talk 2**

A. Listen and sing.

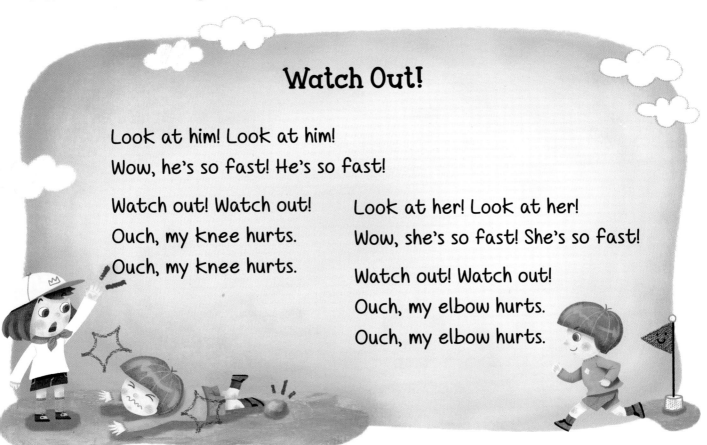

Watch Out!

Look at him! Look at him!
Wow, he's so fast! He's so fast!

Watch out! Watch out!
Ouch, my knee hurts.
Ouch, my knee hurts.

Look at her! Look at her!
Wow, she's so fast! She's so fast!

Watch out! Watch out!
Ouch, my elbow hurts.
Ouch, my elbow hurts.

B. Look, listen, and repeat.

Watch out!

Ouch, my knee hurts.

C. Listen and point. Make sentences.

Ouch, my _____ hurts.

1

arm

2

elbow

3

head

4

knee

A: Watch out!
B: Ouch, my _____ hurts.

D. Listen, point, and say.

Lesson 18 Actions

 Talk 1

A. Look, listen, and repeat.

Don't worry.

Okay.

 Say and Act

Don't worry.

Okay.

B. Listen, number, and say.

 Talk 2

A. Listen and sing.

Can You Stand Up?

Don't worry. Don't worry.
Okay. Okay.

Can you stand up? Can you stand up?
Yes, I can. Yes, I can.
Great! Great!

Don't worry. Don't worry.
Okay. Okay.

Can you jump? Can you jump?
Yes, I can. Yes, I can.
Great! Great!

Can you stand up?

Yes, I can.

76

C. Listen and point. Make sentences.

Can you _____?

1

jump

2

sit down

3

stand up

4

walk

A: Can you _____?
B: Yes, I can.

D. Listen, point, and say.

The Big Frog's Birthday

A. Look, listen, and repeat.

B. Listen and chant.

C. Listen and number.

The big frog wears a yellow wig.
Today is his birthday. A red hen sings in a nest.
A cub dances on a ball. A fox plays the violin on a box.
A pup hops over a net. A pig hits the pots on a mat.
The big frog's friends sit on a rock and a log.
Everybody is happy.

D. Listen and circle the rhyming words.

1

hen	red	frog	pen

2

sun	bun	mug	hat

 **Play**

A. Listen and chant.

Can You Walk?

Watch out! Watch out!
Ouch, my head hurts.

Can you walk?
Can you walk?
Yes, I can.
Yes, I can.

Watch out! Watch out!
Ouch, my arm hurts.

Can you sit down?
Can you sit down?
Yes, I can.
Yes, I can.

B. Play a game.

A: Watch out!
B: Ouch, my knee hurts.

A: Can you jump?
B: Yes, I can.

Reading Time

You Can Do It

Look at her!
She can jump really high.

Look at him!
He can run really fast.

Can you jump like her?
Can you run fast?

Don't worry. If you practice
a lot, you can do it.

Read and check.

1. The man can run (**a** high   **b** fast).
2. You can jump high if you (**a** practice   **b** walk) a lot.

Assessment Test 2

🎧 Listening

A. Listen and check.

1
2
3

B. Listen and choose O or X.

1 O X
2 O X
3 O X
4 O X
5 O X
6 O X

82

C. Listen and circle.

D. Listen and number.

Reading Read and check.

1

- ◯ Let's play soccer.
- ◯ Let's play badminton.

2

- ◯ I'm nine years old.
- ◯ I'm ten years old.

3

- ◯ I'm thirsty.
- ◯ What do you want?

4

- ◯ I want some coke.
- ◯ I want some apple juice.

5

- ◯ Watch out!
- ◯ Get in line.

6

- ◯ Can you walk?
- ◯ Can you sit down?

Writing Match and trace.

1
 • •  Let's drink some water.

2
 • •  I want bread.

3
 • •  He's my friend.

4
 • • I'm thirsty.

 **Speaking**

A. Listen, point, and answer.

B. Listen and answer.

Syllabus

Lesson	Topic	Language	Key Vocabulary
Lesson 1	Time	What time is it? - It's eight o'clock. Wake up! - Okay, Sally.	six seven eight nine ten
Lesson 2	My Body	Wash your face. - Okay. It's time for school. - Oh, no. I'm late.	face feet hands neck
Lesson 3	Step Up 1	Phonics: -am, -an, -ap, -at Lessons 1~2 Review	Phonics: ham, jam, can, fan, map, nap, hat, mat
Lesson 4	Feelings	What's wrong? - I'm tired. Are you okay? - No, I'm not.	angry sad sleepy tired
Lesson 5	Symptoms	Do you have a fever? -Yes, I do. How do you feel today? - I'm sick.	cold fever headache toothache
Lesson 6	Step Up 2	Phonics: -ed, -en, -et, -est Lessons 4~5 Review	Phonics: bed, red, hen, pen, net, wet, nest, vest
Lesson 7	Days of the Week	What day is it today? - It's Monday. Be quiet. - I'm sorry.	Monday Friday Tuesday Saturday Wednesday Sunday Thursday
Lesson 8	Subjects	Today is Monday. - I like Monday. We have music class. Don't run! - Okay.	art math music P.E.
Lesson 9	Step Up 3	Phonics: -ig, -in, -it, -ix Lessons 7~8 Review	Phonics: big, wig, bin, pin, hit, sit, fix, mix
Lesson 10	Assessment Test 1 Lessons 1~9 Review		

Lesson	Topic	Language	Key Vocabulary
Lesson 11	Cafeteria	What do you want? - I want chicken. Get in line. - Okay.	bread chicken fish rice
Lesson 12	Team Sports	Let's play soccer. - Okay. Look at this, Mark! - Wow, it's a soccer ball!	badminton baseball basketball soccer
Lesson 13	Step Up 4	Phonics: -og, -op, -ot, -ock Lessons 11~12 Review * Reading Time: Foods around the World	Phonics: frog, log, hop, mop, hot, pot, rock, sock
Lesson 14	Playground	Who's that? - He's my coach. How old are you? - I'm eight years old.	coach friend student teacher
Lesson 15	Cold Drinks	Can we drink some water? - Yes, you can. I'm thirsty. - Let's drink some water.	apple juice coke lemonade water
Lesson 16	Step Up 5	Phonics: -ub, -ug, -un, -up Lessons 14~15 Review * Reading Time: Camels in the Desert	Phonics: cub, tub, mug, rug, bun, sun, cup, pup
Lesson 17	Body Parts	Watch out! - Ouch, my knee hurts. Look at him! - Wow, he's so fast!	arm elbow head knee
Lesson 18	Actions	Can you stand up? - Yes, I can. Don't worry. - Okay.	jump sit down stand up walk
Lesson 19	Step Up 6	Phonics Story: The Big Frog's Birthday Lessons 17~18 Review * Reading Time: You Can Do It	Phonics: big, cub, frog, hen, hit, hop, log, mat, nest, net, pot, pup, red, rock, sit, wig
Lesson 20	Assessment Test 2 Lessons 11~19 Review		

Flashcard List

6	six	**7**	seven	**8**	eight
9	nine	**10**	ten		face
	feet		hands		neck
	angry		sad		sleepy
	tired		cold		fever
	headache		toothache	MONDAY	Monday
TUESDAY	Tuesday	WEDNESDAY	Wednesday	THURSDAY	Thursday
FRIDAY	Friday	SATURDAY	Saturday	SUNDAY	Sunday
	art		math		music
	P.E.		bread		chicken
	fish		rice		badminton
	baseball		basketball		soccer
	coach		friend		student
	teacher		apple juice		coke
	lemonade		water		arm
	elbow		head		knee
	jump		sit down		stand up
	walk				

Lesson 1 Time

	Vocabulary	Meaning	Sentence
1	later	나중에	See you later.
2	o'clock	정각	It's eight o'clock.
3	see	보다	See you later.
4	time	시간	What time is it?
5	wake	(잠이) 깨다	Wake up!
6	six	여섯, 6	It's six o'clock.
7	seven	일곱, 7	It's seven o'clock.
8	eight	여덟, 8	It's eight o'clock.
9	nine	아홉, 9	It's nine o'clock.
10	ten	열, 10	It's ten o'clock.

Lesson 2 My Body

	Vocabulary	Meaning	Sentence
1	face	얼굴	Wash your face.
2	feet	발 (foot의 복수형)	Wash your feet.
3	hand	손	Wash your hands.
4	late	늦은	I'm late.
5	neck	목	Wash your neck.
6	okay	알겠어요	Okay.
7	school	학교	It's time for school.
8	time	시간	It's time for school.
9	wash	씻다	Wash your face.
10	your	너의	Wash your feet.

Lesson 5 Symptoms

	Vocabulary	Meaning	Sentence
1	bad	나쁜	Bad.
2	cold	감기	Do you have a cold?
3	feel	느끼다	How do you feel today?
4	good	좋은	Good.
5	fever	열	Do you have a fever?
6	how	어떻게	How do you feel today?
7	headache	두통	Do you have a headache?
8	sick	아픈	I'm sick.
9	today	오늘	How do you feel today?
10	toothache	치통	Do you have a toothache?

Lesson 6 Phonics -ed, -en, -et, -est

	Vocabulary	Meaning	Sentence
1	bed	침대	A red hen is on a bed.
2	egg	달걀, 알	Eight eggs are in a nest.
3	eight	여덟, 8	Eight eggs are in a nest.
4	hen	암탉	A red hen is on a bed.
5	nest	둥지	Eight eggs are in a nest.
6	net	그물 (망)	A red pen is in a net.
7	pen	펜	A red pen is in a net.
8	red	붉은	A red hen is on a bed.
9	vest	조끼	She wears a wet vest.
10	wet	젖은	She wears a wet vest.

Lesson 3 Phonics -am, -an, -ap, -at

	Vocabulary	Meaning	Sentence
1	can	깡통	A can is on a fan.
2	fan	부채	A can is on a fan.
3	ham	햄	A ham is on top of jam.
4	hat	모자	A boy with a hat is on a mat.
5	jam	잼	A ham is on top of jam.
6	map	지도	He takes a nap with a map.
7	mat	매트 (깔개)	A boy with a hat is on a mat.
8	nap	낮잠	He takes a nap with a map.
9	on	~위에	A can is on a fan.
10	top	꼭대기	A ham is on top of jam.

Lesson 4 Feelings

	Vocabulary	Meaning	Sentence
1	angry	화난	I'm angry.
2	hungry	배고픈	Are you hungry?
3	no	아니요	No, I'm not.
4	not	아닌	No, I'm not.
5	okay	괜찮은	Are you okay?
6	sleepy	졸린	I'm sleepy.
7	tired	피곤한	I'm tired.
8	what	무엇	What's wrong?
9	wrong	잘못된	What's wrong?
10	you	너	Are you okay?

Lesson 7 Days of the Week

	Vocabulary	Meaning	Sentence
1	hand	손	Wash your hands.
2	quiet	조용한	Be quiet.
3	wash	씻다	Wash your hands.
4	Monday	월요일	It's Monday.
5	Tuesday	화요일	It's Tuesday.
6	Wednesday	수요일	It's Wednesday.
7	Thursday	목요일	It's Thursday.
8	Friday	금요일	It's Friday.
9	Saturday	토요일	It's Saturday.
10	Sunday	일요일	It's Sunday.

Lesson 8 Subjects

	Vocabulary	Meaning	Sentence
1	art	미술	We have art class.
2	class	수업	We have art class.
3	like	~을 좋아하다	I like Monday.
4	math	수학	We have math class.
5	music	음악	We have music class.
6	oval	타원형	It's an oval.
7	P.E.	체육	We have P.E. class.
8	run	달리다	Don't run.
9	shape	모양	What shape is it?
10	today	오늘	Today is Monday.

Lesson 9 Phonics -ig, -in, -it, -ix

	Vocabulary	Meaning	Sentence
1	big	큰	He has a big wig.
2	bin	쓰레기통	He can sit and fix a bin.
3	dad	아빠	They are my mom and dad.
4	fix	고치다, 고정시키다	He can sit and fix a bin.
5	hit	치다	She can hit and mix eggs.
6	mix	섞다	She can hit and mix eggs.
7	mom	엄마	They are my mom and dad.
8	pin	핀 (압정)	He has a big pin.
9	sit	앉다	He can sit and fix a bin.
10	wig	가발	He has a big wig.

Lesson 11 Cafeteria

	Vocabulary	Meaning	Sentence
1	bread	빵	I want bread.
2	chicken	치킨	I want chicken.
3	fish	생선	I want fish.
4	in	~안에	Get in line.
5	line	줄	Get in line.
6	okay	좋아요	Okay.
7	rice	쌀	I want rice.
8	run	달리다	Don't run.
9	want	원하다	I want bread.
10	what	무엇	What do you want?

Lesson 14 Playground

	Vocabulary	Meaning	Sentence
1	coach	코치	He's my coach.
2	eight	여덟, 8	I'm eight years old.
3	friend	친구	She's my friend.
4	how	얼마나	How old are you?
5	old	나이가 ~인	How old are you?
6	student	학생	She's my student.
7	teacher	선생님	She's my teacher.
8	that	저 사람, 저것	Who's that?
9	who	누구	Who's that?
10	you	너	How old are you?

Lesson 15 Cold Drinks

	Vocabulary	Meaning	Sentence
1	apple juice	사과주스	Can we drink some apple juice?
2	can	~할 수 있다	Yes, you can.
3	coke	콜라	Can we drink some coke?
4	drink	마시다	Let's drink some water.
5	he	그	He's my coach.
6	lemonade	레모네이드	Can we drink some lemonade?
7	my	나의	He's my coach.
8	some	조금, 약간의	Can we drink some apple juice?
9	thirsty	목이 마른	I'm thirsty.
10	water	물	Let's drink some water.

Lesson 12 Team Sports

	Vocabulary	Meaning	Sentence
1	badminton	배드민턴	Let's play badminton.
2	ball	공	Wow, it's a soccer ball!
3	baseball	야구	Let's play baseball.
4	basketball	농구	Let's play basketball.
5	let's	～하자	Let's play badminton.
6	look	보다	Look at this, Mark!
7	play	(운동 경기를) 하다	Let's play baseball.
8	soccer	축구	Let's play soccer.
9	this	이것	Look at this, Mark!
10	wow	와 (놀라움을 나타내는 소리)	Wow, it's a soccer ball!

Lesson 13 Phonics -og, -op, -ot, -ock

	Vocabulary	Meaning	Sentence
1	delicious	맛있는	Oh, all of these look delicious.
2	frog	개구리	A frog is on a log.
3	hop	깡충 뛰다	He can hop with a mop.
4	hot	뜨거운	He can hop with a hot pot.
5	Italian	이탈리아의	It's an Italian food.
6	log	통나무	A frog is on a log.
7	mop	대걸레	He can hop with a mop.
8	pot	냄비	He can hop with a hot pot.
9	rock	바위	A dog is on a rock.
10	sock	양말	She can hop with a sock on.

Lesson 16 Phonics -ub, -ug, -un, -up

	Vocabulary	Meaning	Sentence
1	bun	둥근 빵	Can you see a bun?
2	camel	낙타	It's a camel.
3	cub	(동물의) 새끼	Can you see a cub?
4	cup	컵	The sun is in a cup.
5	mug	머그잔	The bun is in a mug.
6	pup	강아지	Can you see a pup?
7	rug	깔개	The pup is on a rug.
8	sun	태양	Can you see the sun?
9	tub	욕조	The cub is in a tub.
10	without	～없이	Camels can walk for weeks without water.

Lesson 17 Body Parts

	Vocabulary	Meaning	Sentence
1	arm	팔	Ouch, my arm hurts.
2	elbow	팔꿈치	Ouch, my elbow hurts.
3	fast	빠른	Wow, he's so fast!
4	head	머리	Ouch, my head hurts.
5	hurt	다치다	Ouch, my arm hurts.
6	knee	무릎	Ouch, my knee hurts.
7	my	나의	Ouch, my elbow hurts.
8	ouch	아야	Ouch, my head hurts.
9	watch out	조심하다	Watch out!
10	wow	와 (놀라움을 나타내는 소리)	Wow, she's so fast!

	Vocabulary	Meaning	Sentence
1	can	~할 수 있다	Can you jump?
2	don't	~하지 마라	Don't worry.
3	great	훌륭한	Great!
4	head	머리	Ouch, my head hurts.
5	hurt	다치다	Ouch, my head hurts.
6	jump	점프하다	Can you jump?
7	sit down	앉다	Can you sit down?
8	stand up	일어나다	Can you stand up?
9	walk	걷다	Can you walk?
10	worry	걱정하다	Don't worry.

	Vocabulary	Meaning	Sentence
1	big	큰	The big frog wears a yellow wig.
2	frog	개구리	The big frog's friends sit on a rock and a log.
3	hen	암탉	A red hen sings in a nest.
4	high	높이	She can jump really high.
5	if	만약 ~한다면	If you practice a lot, you can do it.
6	practice	연습하다	If you practice a lot, you can do it.
7	really	정말	She can jump really high.
8	red	붉은	A red hen sings in a nest.
9	sing	노래하다	A red hen sings in a nest.
10	wig	가발	The big frog wears a yellow wig.

 **Memo**

 **Memo**

Answers

Student Book Answers

Lesson 1 Time
B. Listen, circle, and say.   p. 7

1. ⓐ   2. ⓑ

Lesson 2 My Body
B. Listen, match, and say.   p. 11

1.

2.

Lesson 3 Phonics -am, -an, -ap, -at
C. Find and circle. Read along.   p. 15

Fun Time   pp. 16~17

1. Wake up!   3. feet

6. It's eight o'clock.   7.

8. Oh, no. I'm late.   9. Wash your hands.

12. It's eight o'clock.

14. What time is it?   15. Wash your feet.

Lesson 4 Feelings
B. Listen, check, and say.   p. 19

1. ⓐ   2. ⓑ

Lesson 5 Symptoms
B. Listen, number, and say.   p. 23

  4   2

 1   3

Lesson 6 Phonics -ed, -en, -et, -est
C. Find and circle. Read along.   p. 27

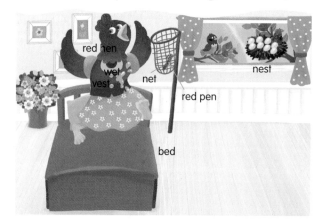

Fun Time   pp. 28~29

1. What's wrong?   5. No, I'm not.

6. sleepy   7. I'm sick.

9. No, I'm not.

10. Do you have a toothache?

11. How do you feel today?

14.   15. Yes, I do.

Lesson 7 Days of the Week
B. Listen, circle, and say.   p. 31

1. ⓐ   2. ⓑ

Lesson 8 Subjects
B. Listen, number, and say.   p. 35

Lesson 9 Phonics -ig, -in, -it, -ix
C. Find and circle. Read along.   p. 39

big wig
big pin
fix
sit
bin
hit
mix

Fun Time   pp. 40~41

1. Be quiet.   **4.** Wednesday

6. Don't run!   **7.**

8. It's Tuesday.   **10.** We have music class.

13. Today is Monday.

14. We have art class.

15. We have math class.

Lesson 10 Assessment Test 1

pp. 42~43

A. 1.   **2.**   **3.**

B. 1. ✕   **2.** ○   **3.** ○   **4.** ✕   **5.** ✕   **6.** ○

C. 1.   **2.**   **3.**

4.   **5.**   **6.**

D.

③   ②   ①   ④

Reading   p. 44

 6   5   1

 3   4   2

Writing   p. 44

1. • — • It's Tuesday.

2. Wash your hands.

3. I'm sad.

4. • — • It's time for school.

Speaking   p. 45

A. 1. It's Friday.   **2.** It's ten o'clock.
    3. I'm sorry.   **4.** Yes, I do.
    5. I'm sick.   **6.** I'm sleepy.

B. 1. I'm tired.   **2.** It's six o'clock.
    3. Oh, no. I'm late.   **4.** Yes, I do.

Lesson 19 The Big Frog's Birthday

C. Listen and number. p. 78

4 2 3 1

D. Listen and circle the rhyming words. p. 79

1. pen 2. bun

Reading Time p. 81

1. ⓑ 2. ⓐ

Lesson 20 Assessment Test 2

pp. 82~83

A. 1.   2.   3.

B. 1. ✕ 2. ○ 3. ○ 4. ○ 5. ✕ 6. ○

C. 1.   2.   3.

4.   5.   6.

D.

4 2 3 1

Reading p. 84

1. Let's play soccer.

2. I'm nine years old.

3. What do you want?

4. I want some apple juice.

5. Get in line.

6. Can you sit down?

Writing p. 84

1. Let's drink some water.

2. I want bread.

3. He's my friend.

4. I'm thirsty.

Speaking p. 85

A. 1. Let's drink some water.

2. Yes, you can.

3. Ouch, my knee hurts.

4. I want apple juice.

5. He's my coach.

6. Wow, he's so fast!

B. 1. I'm seven years old.

2. I want fish.

3. He's my friend.

4. Yes, you can.

Workbook Answers

Lesson 1 Time
pp. 4~5

A. 1. ⓐ Wake up!

ⓑ Okay, Sally.

2. ⓐ What time is it?

ⓑ It's eight o'clock.

B. 2. ⓑ

C.  What time is it?

1. It's six o'clock.

2. It's ten o'clock.

3. It's nine o'clock.

4. It's eight o'clock.

Lesson 2 My Body
pp. 6~7

A. 1. ⓐ It's time for school.

ⓑ Oh, no. I'm late.

2. ⓐ Okay.

ⓑ Wash your face.

B. 2. ⓐ

C. 1. Wash your neck.

2. Wash your feet.

3. Wash your face.

4. Wash your hands.

Lesson 3 Phonics -am, -an, -ap, -at
pp. 8~9

A. 1. -ap

2. -am

3. -an

4. -at

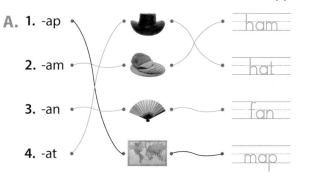

ham

hat

fan

map

100

B. 1.  mat   2.  nap

3. can   4. jam

C. 2. 3. 4.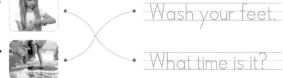

D.
1.   Wash your feet.

2.   What time is it?

3.   Wake up!

4.   It's ten o'clock.

Lesson 4 Feelings   pp. 10~11

A. 1. ⓐ No, I'm not.

ⓑ Are you okay?

2. ⓐ I'm tired.

ⓑ What's wrong?

B. 1. ⓑ   2. ⓐ

C. 1. I'm angry.   I'm angry.

2. I'm tired.   I'm tired.

3. I'm sleepy.   I'm sleepy.

4. I'm sad.   I'm sad.

Lesson 5 Symptoms   pp. 12~13

A. 1. ⓐ How do you feel today?

ⓑ I'm sick.

2. ⓐ Do you have a fever?

ⓑ Yes, I do.

B. 1. ⓐ   2. ⓑ

C. 1. Do you have a fever?   No, I don't.

2. Do you have a cold?   Yes, I do.

3. Do you have a headache?   Yes, I do.

4. Do you have a toothache?   No, I don't.

Lesson 6 Phonics -ed, -en, -et, -est

pp. 14~15

A. 1. -ed (-est) ———— vest

2. -en (-et) ———— pen

3. (-en) -est ———— net

4. (-ed) -et ———— bed

B. 1. r e s d l g h (n e s t) g e r

2. s a e g o (r e d e n) w e t

3. (s h e n) h o n e t k e b e

4. d o x e w e r i c e (w e t)

C. 2. ○   3. ○   4. ○

D. 1. I'm tired.   I'm tired.

2. I have a fever.   I have a fever.

3. I'm sleepy.   I'm sleepy.

4. Are you okay?   Are you okay?

Lesson 7 Days of the Week

pp. 16~17

A. 1. ⓐ Be quiet.

ⓑ I'm sorry.

2. ⓐ What day is it today?

ⓑ It's Monday.

B. 1. ⓑ   2. ⓐ

C. 1. ⓓ It's Monday.

2. ⓔ It's Tuesday.

3. ⓖ It's Wednesday.

4. ⓕ It's Thursday.

5. ⓒ It's Friday.

6. ⓑ It's Saturday.

7. ⓐ It's Sunday.

Lesson 8 Subjects

pp. 18~19

A. 1. ⓐ Okay.

ⓑ Don't run!

2. ⓐ  Today is Monday.

ⓑ  I like Monday. We have music class.

B. 1. Don't run!　　　**2.** Be quiet.

C. 1. 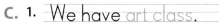 We have art class.

2. We have music class.

3. We have P.E. class.

4.  We have math class.

Lesson 9 Phonics -ig, -in, -it, -ix　　pp. 20~21

A. 1. -ig　　　　　　　hit

2. -it　　　　　　　bin

3. -ix　　　　　　　mix

4. -in　　　　　　　wig

B. 1. big　　**2.** pin

3. fix　　**4.** sit

C.

D. 1. · It's Tuesday.

2. · We have math class.

3. · Be quiet.

4. · Don't run!

Lesson 11 Cafeteria　　pp. 22~23

A. 1. ⓐ Okay.

ⓑ Get in line.

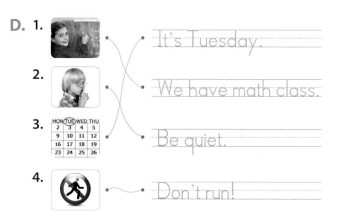

2. ⓐ What do you want?

ⓑ I want chicken.

B. 1. ⓑ　　**2.** ⓐ

C. 1. I want rice.　　○

2. I want chicken.　　×

3. I want fish.　　×

4. I want bread.　　○

Lesson 12 Team Sports

pp. 24~25

A. 1. ⓐ Look at this, Mark!

ⓑ Wow, it's a soccer ball!

2. ⓐ Okay.

ⓑ Let's play soccer.

B. 1. Wash your hands.   2. Wow, it's a soccer ball!

C. 1.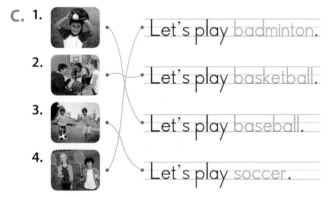

Let's play badminton.

2. Let's play basketball.

3. Let's play baseball.

4. Let's play soccer.

Lesson 13 Phonics -og, -op, -ot, -ock

pp. 26~27

A. 1. -ot

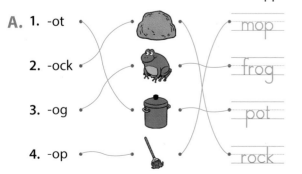

mop

2. -ock

frog

3. -og

pot

4. -op

rock

B. 1. b a o n o g e h o p x w

2. l o g p i g s e k s o k h

3. h o c a n u r h o t p o i

4. m a s o c k i g m o n t

C. 1. ⓐ I want fish.

2. ⓐ What do you want?

3. ⓐ Let's play soccer.

4. ⓑ Okay.

D. 1. delicious • • pasta

2. Indian • • Indian

3. Mexican • • delicious

4. pasta • • Mexican

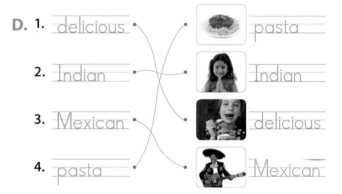

Lesson 14 Playground

pp. 28~29

A. 1. ⓐ I'm eight years old.

ⓑ How old are you?

2. ⓐ Who's that?

ⓑ He's my coach.

B. **1.** Look at this, Mark!
  2. I'm eight years old.

C. **1.** She's my student.   ○

  2. He's my teacher.   ×

  3. She's my friend.   ×

  4. He's my coach.   ○

Lesson 15 Cold Drinks   pp. 30~31

A. **1.** ⓐ I'm thirsty.

  ⓑ Let's drink some water.

  2. ⓐ Yes, you can.

  ⓑ Can we drink some water?

B. **1.** ⓑ   **2.** ⓐ

C. **1.** apple juice   **2.** lemonade

  3. water   **4.** coke

Lesson 16 Phonics -ub, -ug, -un, -up   pp. 32~33

A. **1.**  bun   **2.**  cub

  3.  mug   **4.** cup

B. **1.** -ub
  2. -un
  3. -ug
  4. -up

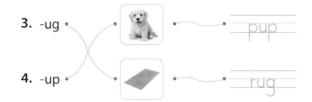

  sun
  tub
  pup
  rug

C. **1.** She's my teacher.

  2. Can we drink some water?

  3. He's my friend.

  4. Who's that?

 2   1   4   3

D. **1.** camel camel

  2. desert desert

  3. that that

  4. hump hump

Lesson 17 Body Parts

pp. 34~35

A. 1. ⓐ Look at him!

ⓑ Wow, he's so fast!

2. ⓐ Watch out!

ⓑ Ouch, my knee hurts.

B. 1. ⓑ   **2.** ⓑ

C. 1. Ouch, my knee hurts.

2. Ouch, my arm hurts.

3. Ouch, my elbow hurts.

4. Ouch, my head hurts.

Lesson 18 Actions

pp. 36~37

A. 1. ⓐ Okay.

ⓑ Don't worry.

2. ⓐ Can you stand up?

ⓑ Yes, I can.

B. 1. ⓑ   **2.** ⓐ

C. 1. Can you jump?

 ↑ 2

2. Can you stand up?

 4

3. Can you sit down?

 ↓ 3

4. Can you walk?

 1

Lesson 19 The Big Frog's Birthday

pp. 38~39

A. 1. -un

2. -og

3. -ug

4. -in

5. -ed

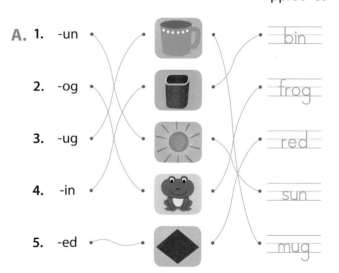

bin

frog

red

sun

mug

B.
1. -ig   wig
2. -at   hat
3. -ock   rock
4. -up   pup
5. -en   pen

C.

2   Watch out!

3   Ouch, my knee hurts.

4   Ouch, my arm hurts.

1   Can you jump?

D.
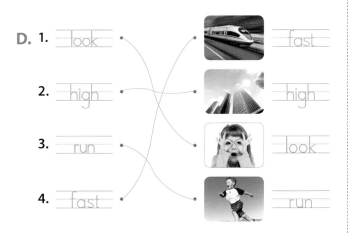
1. look   fast
2. high   high
3. run   look
4. fast   run

Final Test
English Town Starter Book 2

1. ②	2. ⑤	3. ②	4. ④	5. ①
6. ④	7. ③	8. ⑤	9. ①	10. ②
11. ⑤	12. ③	13. ③	14. ②	15. ②
16. ③	17. ③	18. ④	19. have	

20. Wednesday   class

Memo

Final Test_English Town Starter Book 2

Part 3 - Reading

13 Read and choose the right word.

> **A:** Watch out!
> **B:** Ouch, my knee _____.

① wash   ② have   ③ hurts
④ drink   ⑤ angry

14 Read and choose the right answer.

> **A:** Can you walk?
> **B:** _____

① I'm sad.   ② Yes, I can.
③ I want rice.   ④ It's nine o'clock.
⑤ No, I'm not.

[17-18] Read and answer the questions.

> **A:** I'm thirsty.
> **B:** Let's drink some apple juice.
> **A:** Mom, _____ we drink some
>   apple juice?
> **C:** Yes, you can.

17 What is the right word for the blank?

① is   ② are   ③ can
④ how   ⑤ what

18 What do **A** and **B** want to drink?

①   ②   ③

Final Test

English Town Starter Book 2

Class	Name	Score
		/20

[1-2] Listen and choose the rhyming word.

1

① ② ③ ④ ⑤

2

① ② ③ ④ ⑤

[3-4] Listen and choose the right picture.

3

① ②  ③

[7-8] Listen and choose the right picture.

7

①  ②  ③

④ ⑤

8

① ②  ③

④ ⑤

[9-10] Listen and choose the right conversation

④

for the picture.

4　① 　② 6　③ 7　④ 9　⑤ 10

[5-6] Listen and choose the right sentence for the picture.

5
① ② ③ ④ ⑤

6
① ② ③ ④ ⑤

9
① ② ③ ④ ⑤

10
① ② ③ ④ ⑤

Part 2 - Speaking

11　Listen and choose the correct conversation.
① ② ③ ④ ⑤

12　Listen and choose the best response.
① Wake up!　② I'm late.
③ I'm sick.　④ Yes, I do.
⑤ Watch out!

[15-16] Read and answer the questions.

A: _____ time for school.
B: Oh, no. I'm late.
A: Wash your face.
B: Okay.

15 What is the right word for the blank?
　① I'm　② It's　③ He's
　④ She's　⑤ You're

16 What will B do after the conversation?

① 　② 　③

④ 　⑤

[19-20] Choose and write the right word.

| class | sick | have | Wednesday |

19 A: Do you _____ a toothache?
　　B: Yes, I do.

20 A: Today is Wednesday.
　　B: I like _____.
　　　 We have art _____.

ENGLISH TOWN

FOR EVERYONE

STARTER

BOOK

2

WORKBOOK

Contents

Lesson **1** **Time**

A. Trace and choose.

1
ⓐ Wake up!

ⓑ Okay, Sally.

2
ⓐ What time is it?

ⓑ It's eight o'clock.

B. Read and match.

1

 **ⓐ** See you later.

2

ⓑ Wake up!

C. Trace and draw.

What time is it?

1 It's six o'clock.

2 It's ten o'clock.

3 It's nine o'clock.

4 It's eight o'clock.

Lesson 2 My Body

A. Trace and choose.

1
  ⓐ It's time for school.

  ⓑ Oh, no. I'm late.

2
  ⓐ Okay.

  ⓑ Wash your face.

B. Read and circle.

1

    ⓐ Goodbye.

    ⓑ It's time for school.

2

    ⓐ Oh, no. I'm late.

    ⓑ Wake up!

C. Trace and match.

1 Wash your neck. •   •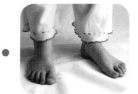

2 Wash your feet. •   •

3 Wash your face. •   •

4 Wash your hands. •   •

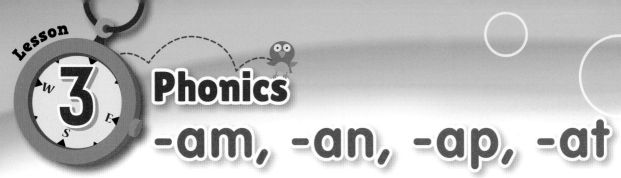

Phonics
-am, -an, -ap, -at

A. Match and trace.

1 -ap

2 -am

3 -an

4 -at

ham

hat

fan

map

B. Circle and trace.

1 -at   mat

2 -ap   nap

3 -an   can

4 -am   jam

C. Read and check.

1 A: Wake up!
B: Okay.

 ☐  ✓

2 A: It's time for school.
B: Oh, no. I'm late.

 ☐  ☐

3 A: What time is it?
B: It's eight o'clock.

 ☐  ☐

4 A: Wash your neck.
B: Okay.

 ☐  ☐

D. Match and trace.

1  •

• Wash your feet.

2  •

• What time is it?

3  •

• Wake up!

4  •

• It's ten o'clock.

A. Trace and choose.

1
  a No, I'm not.

  b Are you okay?

2
  a I'm tired.

  b What's wrong?

B. Read and match.

1

•

• **ⓐ** A: Are you hungry?
B: Yes, I am.

2

•

• **ⓑ** A: Are you okay?
B: No, I'm not.

C. Check and trace.

1 ☐ I'm angry.
☐ I'm tired.

I'm angry.

2 ☐ I'm sad.
☐ I'm tired.

I'm tired.

3 ☐ I'm angry.
☐ I'm sleepy.

I'm sleepy.

4  ☐ I'm sad.
☐ I'm sleepy.

I'm sad.

Symptoms

A. Trace and choose.

1
  a How do you feel today?

  b I'm sick.

2
  a Do you have a fever?

  b Yes, I do.

B. Read and circle.

1   A: How do you feel today?
    B: I'm sad.

    a    b

2   A: How do you feel today?
    B: I'm sick.

    a    b

C. Trace and check.

1   Do you have a fever?      ☐ Yes, I do.   ☑ No, I don't.

2   Do you have a cold?      ☐ Yes, I do.   ☐ No, I don't.

3   Do you have a headache?   ☐ Yes, I do.   ☐ No, I don't.

4   Do you have a toothache?   ☐ Yes, I do.   ☐ No, I don't.

Phonics
-ed, -en, -et, -est

A. Circle and trace.

1 -ed (-est) · · vest

2 -en -et · · pen

3 -en -est · · net

4 -ed -et · · bed

B. Find and circle.

 gih(ama)lelter

1 resdlghnestger

2 saegoredenwet

3 shenhonetkebe

4 doxewericewet

C. Read and choose O or X.

1

A: What's wrong?
B: I'm angry.

O Ⓧ

2

A: How do you feel today?
B: I'm sick.

O X

3

A: Are you okay?
B: No, I'm not.

O X

4

A: Do you have a headache?
B: Yes, I do.

O X

D. Check and trace.

1

☐ I'm angry.
☐ I'm tired.

I'm tired.

2

☐ I have a fever.
☐ I have a toothache.

I have a fever.

3

☐ I'm sad.
☐ I'm sleepy.

I'm sleepy.

4

☐ Are you okay?
☐ Wash your face.

Are you okay?

A. Trace and choose.

1
  a Be quiet.
  b I'm sorry.

2
  a What day is it today?
  b It's Monday.

B. Read and circle.

1

Be quiet.

ⓐ I'm sad.

ⓑ I'm sorry.

2

How do you feel today?

ⓐ I'm sick.

ⓑ I'm angry.

C. Match and trace.

1   MONDAY •

2   TUESDAY •

3   WEDNESDAY •

4   THURSDAY •

5   FRIDAY •

6   SATURDAY •

7   SUNDAY •

• ⓐ It's Sunday.

• ⓑ It's Saturday.

• ⓒ It's Friday.

• ⓓ It's Monday.

• ⓔ It's Tuesday.

• ⓕ It's Thursday.

• ⓖ It's Wednesday.

Lesson **8** **Subjects**

A. Trace and choose.

1
   a Okay.

   b Don't run!

2
   a Today is Monday.

   b I like Monday. We have music class.

B. Read and check.

○ Don't run!
○ I'm sorry.

○ Okay.
○ Be quiet.

C. Trace and match.

1 We have art class. •

2 We have music class. •

3 We have P.E. class. •

4 We have math class. •

Phonics
-ig, -in, -it, -ix

A. Match and trace.

1 -ig •  • hit

2 -it •  • bin

3 -ix •  • mix

4 -in •  • wig

B. Circle and trace.

1 -ig    big

2 -in   pin

3 -ix   fix

4 -it   sit

C. Read and check.

1 A: Be quiet.
B: I'm sorry.

 ○  ○

2 A: What day is it today?
B: It's Sunday.

 ○  ○

3 A: Don't run!
B: Okay.

 ○  ○

4 A: Today is Monday.
B: I like Monday.
We have art class.

 ○  ○

D. Match and trace.

1  •

2  •

• It's Tuesday.

• We have math class.

3  •

4  •

• Be quiet.

• Don't run!

11 Cafeteria

A. Trace and choose.

1.
  ⓐ Okay.
  ⓑ Get in line.

2.
  ⓐ What do you want?
  ⓑ I want chicken.

B. Read and circle.

1 Get in line.

2 Don't run!

C. Trace and choose O or X.

1 I want rice.   O   X

2 I want chicken.   O   X

3 I want fish.   O   X

4 I want bread.   O   X

12 Team Sports

A. Trace and choose.

1
 ⓐ Look at this, Mark!

 ⓑ Wow, it's a soccer ball!

2
 ⓐ Okay.

 ⓑ Let's play soccer.

B. Read and check.

1

○ We have P.E. class.
○ Wash your hands.

2

○ Get in line.
○ Wow, it's a soccer ball!

C. Match and trace.

1  •

• Let's play badminton.

2  •

• Let's play basketball.

3  •

• Let's play baseball.

4  •

• Let's play soccer.

Phonics
-og, -op, -ot, -ock

A. Match and trace.

1 -ot

2 -ock

3 -og

4 -op

mop

frog

pot

rock

B. Find and circle.

1 baonogehopxw

2 logpigseksokh

3 hocanurhotpoi

4 masockigmont

C. Circle and trace.

1
   ⓐ I want fish.
   ⓑ I want rice.

I want fish.

2
   ⓐ What do you want?
   ⓑ What day is it toady?

What do you want?

3
   ⓐ Let's play soccer.
   ⓑ Let's play basketball.

Let's play soccer.

4
   ⓐ Sorry.
   ⓑ Okay.

Okay.

D. Trace, match, and rewrite.

1 delicious •

•

2 Indian •

•

3 Mexican •

•  delicious

4 pasta •

•

Lesson 14 Playground

A. Trace and choose.

1
  a I'm eight years old.

  b How old are you?

2
  a Who's that?

  b He's my coach.

B. Read and check.

1

○ Look at this, Mark!

○ How old are you?

2

○ I'm sick.

○ I'm eight years old.

C. Trace and choose O or X.

1 She's my student.  O X

2 He's my teacher.  O X

3 She's my friend.  O X

4 He's my coach.  O X

15 Cold Drinks

A. Trace and choose.

1
  a I'm thirsty.

  b Let's drink some water.

2
  a Yes, you can.

  b Can we drink some water?

B. Read and match.

- •

- • **ⓐ** I want chicken.

- •

- • **ⓑ** Let's drink some water.

C. Check and trace.

 Can we drink some _____?

1  ○ apple juice ○ water

2  ○ coke ○ lemonade

3  ○ apple juice ○ water

4  ○ coke ○ lemonade

Phonics
-ub, -ug, -un, -up

A. Circle and trace.

1 -un   bun

2 -ub  cub

3 -ug   mug

4 -up   cup

B. Match and trace.

1 -ub •  • sun

2 -un •  • tub

3 -ug •  • pup

4 -up •  • rug

32

C. Trace and number.

1 She's my teacher.

2 Can we drink some water?

3 He's my friend.

4 Who's that?

D. Trace, circle, and rewrite.

1 camel

camel

2 desert

3 that

4 hump

Lesson 17 Body Parts

A. Trace and choose.

1 ⓐ Look at him!

ⓑ Wow, he's so fast!

2 ⓐ Watch out!

ⓑ Ouch, my knee hurts.

B. Read and circle.

1

    a Oh, no. I'm late.

    b Wow, she's so fast!

2

    a How old are you?

    b Can we drink some water?

C. Trace and match.

1 Ouch, my knee hurts. •

2 Ouch, my arm hurts. •

3 Ouch, my elbow hurts. •

4 Ouch, my head hurts. •

18 Actions

A. Trace and choose.

1
a Okay.

b Don't worry.

2
a Can you stand up?

b Yes, I can.

B. Read and match.

•

• **a** Don't worry.

•

• **b** Look at her!

C. Trace and number.

1 Can you jump?

2 Can you stand up?

3 Can you sit down?

4 Can you walk?

The Big Frog's Birthday

A. Match and trace.

1 -un •

2 -og •

3 -ug •

4 -in •

5 -ed •

bin

frog

red

sun

mug

B. Circle and trace.

1 -in   -ix   -ig   -it   wig

2 -at   -ap   -an   -am   hat

3 -op   -ock   -ot   -og   rock

4 -un   -ug   -up   -ub   pup

5 -ed   -en   -et   -est   pen

C. Number and write.

1 Can you jump?   2 Watch out!
3 Ouch, my knee hurts.   4 Ouch, my arm hurts.

☐ Watch out!

☐ Ouch, my _____ hurts.

☐ Ouch, my _____ hurts.

☐ Can you jump?

D. Trace, match, and rewrite.

1 look •

2 high •

3 run •

4 fast •

look

Memo

ENGLiSH TOWN STARTER

ENGLiSH TOWN STARTER BOOK 2

English Town is a spoken English course comprised of a series of 9 books, specifically designed for elementary school students.

- Learning English in a communicative way and in an easy manner
- Focused approach to new words, expressions, and dialogs
- Fun to sing and chant together
- Simple but effective games and activities
- Exciting stories

Components

· Student Book

· Workbook

· Final Test

· Teacher's Guide including teaching resources

· Online (www.ybmenglishtown.com)

  Interactive e-book for teachers and students

  E-learning for self-study

 www.ybmenglishtown.com

YBM